Original title:
The Frozen Flame

Copyright © 2024 Swan Charm
All rights reserved.

Author: Sabrina Sarvik
ISBN HARDBACK: 978-9916-79-684-9
ISBN PAPERBACK: 978-9916-79-685-6
ISBN EBOOK: 978-9916-79-686-3

Burning Below the Ice

Whispers hide beneath the cold,
A warmth that flickers, yet untold.
Frozen layers, secrets keep,
Burning hearts in winter's sleep.

Glimmers dance through icy seams,
Unseen fire, chasing dreams.
Shadows flicker, warmth remains,
Beneath the frost, a fire reigns.

The chill wraps tight around the flame,
A silent song, without a name.
Ice encircles, holds it tight,
Yet deep within, it yearns for light.

In moments still, the world stands bare,
A testament to warmth we share.
Duality of hot and cold,
A story of the brave and bold.

Through the frost, the echoes call,
Burning whispers, breaking thrall.
Nature's dance of fire and ice,
In every heart, a sacrifice.

Spark of a Snowstorm

In the sky, a spark ignites,
Whirling winds in winter nights.
Silent chaos starts to grow,
Each flake dances, falling slow.

Fires hidden in the white,
Flickers of warmth bring delight.
Though the storm may howl and rage,
Beauty lives on nature's page.

A gentle touch, a fleeting kiss,
Snowflakes fall, a moment's bliss.
The spark ignites the swirling dance,
Creating magic, given chance.

Through the storm, bright embers glow,
Life beneath the crystal show.
Each gust carries dreams so near,
In the chaos, love appears.

As the tempest weaves its song,
We'll find where our hearts belong.
In frosty realms, warmth starts to bloom,
A spark within the winter's gloom.

Chilling Radiance

In the dusk, the stars align,
Radiant glow, so cold, divine.
Chilling beauty fills the air,
Light that dances everywhere.

Frosted whispers touch the ground,
Every sparkle, magic found.
Silent nights with dreams untold,
The chilling radiance unfolds.

In shadowy corners, secrets lie,
Softly twinkling in the sky.
A heart that beats in winter's breath,
Creating warmth that defies death.

Waves of cold, yet warmth implies,
A secret kept within the skies.
Embers pulse beneath the chill,
Radiance whispers, hearts they fill.

In every flake that softly falls,
Is a story that gently calls.
Wrapped in night, a tender glow,
Chilling radiance starts to flow.

Fire's Shiver

In the hearth, the embers play,
Flickering with a bright display.
Warmth envelops, yet it shivers,
A dance of flames that softly quivers.

Beneath the ashes, sparks reside,
Hiding where the shadows hide.
Breath of fire, silent as night,
Fighting back against the blight.

As winds of winter swirl around,
The heart of fire must be found.
In every spark, a story stirs,
A testament to life's full purrs.

Embers pulse within the dark,
Every flicker, every spark.
Table set for tales to tell,
Where fire's shiver casts its spell.

In the echoes of the night,
Is the warmth of love's pure light.
Fire's shiver, tender embrace,
Uniting souls in time and space.

Chill of a Lingering Spark

In the silence, whispers stir,
Faint embers dance, a soft allure.
Breath of winter, crisp and clear,
Lingering warmth, though far, is near.

Branches bare, yet shadows stay,
A flicker hints of brighter day.
Petals closed, hearts still aflame,
In the cold, we feel the same.

Stars above, a silver thread,
Memory's warmth never quite dead.
Chill lives on, yet hope won't part,
In every frost, there beats a heart.

Frostbitten Passion

In the night, the frost takes hold,
Secrets whispered, passions bold.
Ice-bound dreams, like shadows, creep,
Through the night, our souls do leap.

Breath held tight in winter's clutch,
Yearning hearts, we crave the touch.
Fingers frozen, yet still we fight,
In the dark, we seek the light.

Stars that sparkle, reflecting heat,
In the cold, our pulses meet.
Frostbitten, yet fiercely alive,
In this chill, our passions thrive.

Glacial Glow

Beneath the moon, a silver sheen,
Where ice and fire softly glean.
Hearts entwined in glacial flow,
Warmth ignites from cold's deep throe.

Crystals dancing, light reframed,
With every spark, our love proclaimed.
Through the night, we share our breath,
In this glow, defying death.

Winds may howl, and shadows loom,
Yet in the dark, our spirits bloom.
With every chill, our flames will rise,
In glacial moments, love defies.

Heart of the Winter's Fire

Beneath the snow, a fire gleams,
Born from hope, alive in dreams.
Firesides crackle, warmth embraced,
In winter's breath, our love is traced.

Against the frost, our sparks ignite,
Wrapped in warmth, we chase the night.
Blazing souls in winter's chill,
Hearts collide, a fire still.

Embers glow in darkest hours,
Together strong, we bloom like flowers.
In the heart of winter's fire,
Love will soar, and never tire.

Ashen Dreams in Frost

Beneath the pale, cold sky, they lie,
Whispers of a world once bright.
Frosted hopes in silver sigh,
Hidden where the shadows bite.

Silent echoes of time past,
Glimmers of a fading spark.
A fleeting warmth is outclassed,
In the stillness, all is dark.

Veiled in white, the dreams do creep,
Across the fields, both wide and vast.
In the silence, secrets keep,
Held in the chill that cannot last.

Frozen waters still their flow,
Beneath a shroud of icy gloom.
Where none can hear the softest low,
Heartbeats lost to winter's tomb.

Ashen dreams on winds do sail,
Through the night, a gentle toll.
In the frost, we hear their wail,
A hollow cry of restless soul.

Flickering in the Ice

Stars reflect on frosted panes,
Dancing whispers of the night.
A shivering balm, like soft refrains,
Breath is fog in silvery light.

A lantern glows with tender care,
Casting shadows on the ground.
In the stillness, hearts laid bare,
Hopes of warmth are softly found.

Through barren trees, a sigh winds chase,
Branches coated, pale and bright.
Frozen stillness gives us space,
In the chill, we find our light.

Cracking ice beneath the feet,
A brittle song of nature's jest.
Moments fleeting, yet so sweet,
Beneath the frost, we dare to rest.

Flickering flames in the cold night,
Reminding us we're not alone.
Even in this crisp twilight,
Love can thrive, like seeds we've sown.

Winter's Passion

A flurry drapes the world in white,
Soft caress, a lover's kiss.
With every breath, we hold tight,
To warmth that whispers, "You are missed."

Branches bow with weighty coats,
Every flake tells a tale untold.
Silent love in frozen moats,
Glimmers softly in the cold.

Starlit skies guide hearts anew,
Burning bright in the deep expanse.
In the frost, we're born to do,
Finding joy in every dance.

Chill bites at our fingertips,
Yet close we draw, in shadows' sway.
In this frost, our courage lifts,
As winter claims both night and day.

Winter wraps us in its grace,
A sigh exchanged, then fading fast.
Hand in hand, we find our place,
In this moment, true love's cast.

Heat Beneath the Frost

Glimmers dance on icy shores,
Underneath, the fire stirs.
Buried deep, a longing pours,
Dancing softly, heart's soft purrs.

In the cold, resilience grows,
Roots entwined beneath the frost.
Amidst the ice, our courage glows,
Through the chill, we seek the lost.

A flame ignites in hushed delight,
Filling shadows with warm light.
Even when the world is slight,
Hope endures through darkest plight.

Winter's grip cannot restrain,
What thrives beneath the surface hard.
Through every trial, love remains,
In the warmth, our souls are scarred.

Heat beneath, in stillness found,
Life persists with fervent grace.
In each heart, a pulse profound,
Defying ice, we find our place.

Beneath the Frost's Veil

Beneath the frost's cold veil,
Whispers of winter prevail.
Silent dreams in icy glow,
Nature's breath, steady and slow.

Boughs heavy with sparkling white,
Stars above in deepening night.
Footprints vanish, quiet tread,
In the hush, the world is wed.

Trees sigh under frosty weight,
Branches bow as if in state.
Moonlight dances, shadows play,
Silent serenade till day.

Morning breaks with golden hue,
Frosted fields greet sun anew.
The chill recedes, warmth draws near,
Nature thaws, the path is clear.

Underneath the soft white sea,
Life persists, a mystery.
Beneath the frost, hope resides,
In winter's heart, spring abides.

Glare of the Frozen Ember

In the glare of frozen light,
Embers flicker, bold and bright.
Chill surrounds the glowing fire,
Hearts are warm beneath desire.

Crystals shine like stars at dawn,
Bright against the frosted lawn.
Whispers of warmth, secrets kept,
In coldness where the lovers wept.

The flame's dance, a fleeting spark,
Chasing shadows in the dark.
Frosted breath on lashes freeze,
A moment captured in the breeze.

Glistening dreams like diamond tears,
Woven tight through frigid years.
In the night, the spirit glows,
Amidst the chill, the fire grows.

From embers rise the hopes anew,
In the frost, a vibrant hue.
Each flicker holds a story dear,
In the glare, love's path is clear.

Combustion in the Cold

In winter's clutch, the heart ignites,
Combustion blooms on frigid nights.
Each breath a cloud, a ghostly sigh,
Passion burns where dreams comply.

Fires crackle, warmth unsealed,
In icy grasp, our fate revealed.
Shadows dance on frosty glass,
In every spark, sweet moments pass.

Fingers clasped, the world a blur,
In the chaos, the heart can stir.
Outside, the cold winds howl and bite,
Yet here, within, it's pure delight.

Burning embers, secrets told,
In this maze of winter's hold.
Ignition of a love so bold,
Combustion in the cold unfolds.

In the silence, hearts ignite,
Two souls clash, creating light.
A flicker in the darkened dim,
Combustion rises, passion's hymn.

Glacial Inferno

In the glacial inferno's might,
Heat and cold in fierce delight.
Flames leap forth, with icy breath,
A paradox that dances with death.

Sparks that fly through frozen air,
Passion raging, fierce and rare.
Frigid winds wrap 'round the flame,
A wild dance that knows no shame.

Frozen lakes reflect the fire,
Nature's clash, a fierce desire.
Elements in woven fight,
Dusk and dawn, they dance in light.

From the frost, the heat will rise,
A phoenix born beneath the skies.
In this storm, the worlds collide,
Where glacial waters fiercely slide.

Inferno born of winter's kiss,
In the chaos, find your bliss.
With each heartbeat, worlds unite,
In glacial inferno's wild night.

Frozen Glow of Yearning

In the hush of the night,
Stars glisten like tears,
Whispers of dreams soar,
Dancing with moon's beams.

Chilled winds caress skin,
Brittle branches entice,
Heartbeats echo soft,
Yearning becomes ice.

Distant fires burn bright,
Flickers of hope glint,
In shadows of longing,
Frosted moments hint.

Nature's quiet breath,
Frosted fields awake,
Each glimmering crystal,
A promise we make.

Lasting cold will fade,
With the sun's warm embrace,
Yet till that day comes,
We stay in this space.

The Embered Heart Within Cold

Beneath layers of frost,
A warmth beats in time,
A heart full of ember,
An echo of rhyme.

Ice encloses the soul,
Yet flickers ignite,
With every soft whisper,
A dance with the night.

Shadows silently stretch,
Across valleys of white,
But passion persists,
In the depths of the night.

Winds may sting and bite,
But we cherish the burn,
For winter's embrace,
Is a lesson to learn.

When spring gently calls,
And the cold melts away,
Embers will arise,
To greet a new day.

Sealed in Ice

Silent world wrapped tight,
In blankets of white,
Every breath held captive,
In winter's pure light.

Frozen lakes watch dreams,
As they drift on the shore,
Voices lost in glimmers,
Of what we explore.

Echoes trapped in time,
Moments sealed and stored,
Fragments of our past,
On memories we hoard.

Yet with every heartbeat,
Hope softly sings clear,
Beneath all the layers,
A new dawn draws near.

Though cold hands may grip,
And shadows entwine,
We find strength in yearning,
To break through the line.

Sublime Melting

As winter thaws slowly,
Awakening streams flow,
Tears of joy cascade,
In the sun's gentle glow.

Each droplet's a blessing,
A promise held dear,
Reviving the spirit,
Chasing away fear.

Petals unfurl softly,
In colors so bold,
Spring whispers its magic,
New stories unfold.

Melodies of nature,
In harmony rise,
As the world sheds its chill,
To welcome blue skies.

Life's cycles bring change,
And with every warm breath,
We taste the sublime,
In the dance of life, death.

Burn of the Blizzard

The winds howl like wailing ghosts,
   Snow drapes the darkened trees,
    Each flake a whispered tale,
    Of winter's fierce decrees.

In the depths where shadows creep,
   Cold fingers clutch the night,
    But embers softly glow,
   A dance of warmth and light.

Fire crackles, bright and bold,
   As frost bites at the door,
The heart beats on with courage,
   Longing to feel once more.

Through the white the fire calls,
    A flicker in the gloom,
   It whispers ancient secrets,
   Of spring beyond the tomb.

So stand against the blizzard's rage,
   With spirits fierce and free,
   For in the burn of twilight,
   The warmth will always be.

Glint of Frosted Ash

In twilight's gentle sigh,
The embers softly gleam,
Frosted ash, a secret hope,
A flicker from a dream.

Snowflakes fall like silver stars,
Each one a fleeting spark,
Yet in the cold, we find our way,
A light against the dark.

The night wears a crystal crown,
While shadows steal the breath,
But even here, a glint remains,
Defying winter's death.

Gather round the hearth of hearts,
Feel warmth in every hue,
For in this frost-kissed solitude,
Hope whispers, strong and true.

Let not the chill disguise the flame,
In every lost embrace,
For glints of frosted ash remind,
Of life, and love, and grace.

Warming the Winter's Veil

Beneath the winter's icy shroud,
A warmth begins to rise,
With every flicker, every spark,
It breaks the frozen skies.

The chilling winds may strive to steal,
Joy from each passing breath,
But in the hearth, the flames will heal,
Defying the cold's depth.

Each snowflake dances, swirling light,
A ballet of the night,
Within our hearts the fire fights,
To keep our dreams in sight.

So gather close and share a smile,
In shadows, let love blend,
Through winter's veil, we'll find our way,
Together, till the end.

For warming thoughts and tender words,
Will melt away despair,
In every frosty moment,
A radiant love we share.

Shard of Heat

In frigid nights where silence reigns,
A shard of heat persists,
It flickers like a distant star,
A fire within the mist.

Frost blooms on the windowpanes,
Yet warmth lingers near,
With every crackle of the flame,
Hope whispers in our ear.

From embers deep, a story breathes,
Of life beneath the snow,
Each pulse, a testament to love,
In darkness, watch it grow.

So let the winter have its hold,
We carry light inside,
For in the shard of heat we find,
A love that won't subside.

Through chilling storms and howling nights,
Together, side by side,
With every spark our spirits climb,
In warmth, we shall abide.

Arctic Sizzle

In the frost, warmth does hide,
Waves of heat and ice collide.
Snowflakes dance on fiery breath,
Contradictions near to death.

Silent nights, embers glow,
Frigid winds, a heated show.
Mountains whisper, rivers freeze,
Moments lost in winter's tease.

Fires crackle 'neath the chill,
Hearts ignited against the will.
Nature's pulse, a constant fight,
In the dark, we seek the light.

Beneath the stars, the world is still,
Sizzle echoes, bending will.
Tension mounts, the air is thick,
Craving warmth, another tick.

A dance of frost, a blaze of heat,
Endless cycle, bittersweet.
In this clash of fire and ice,
Love ignites, pays the price.

Cold Embers of Love

In the quiet, embers wane,
Whispers lost, echoing pain.
Chilled affection, over time,
Hearts once warm, now in rhyme.

Frosty mornings, slumber deep,
Secrets shared, yet none to keep.
In pale light, shadows creep,
Love's warmth fades in winter's sweep.

Candles flicker, hearts confined,
Fading spark, the ties unwind.
Silent prayers in the night,
Hope ignites with morning's light.

Beneath layers, heat remains,
Cold embers hold the last refrains.
A flicker here, a sigh out there,
Love's soft glow, now rare to share.

Yet in stillness, dreams abide,
Through the chill, love's hope will ride.
In dark corners, warmth will hover,
Turning cold embers to discover.

Shattered Heat

Once a blaze, now shards of light,
Fragments scattered, lost from sight.
Lightning bursts, the echoes freeze,
Burning passion turned to tease.

In the ashes, memories gleam,
Silent stories, lost in dream.
Sparks that danced now merely sigh,
What was fire, now whispers lie.

Frostbite slips through every crack,
Leaving shadows, taking back.
Time unravels, moments fleet,
Desire fades to bitter sweet.

A shattered heart in icy breath,
Holding onto love's lost depth.
In the dark, a haunting pain,
Reflecting on what might remain.

Yet hope flickers, dim but bold,
In the silence, warmth retold.
Through every shard, a promise glows,
That love, once shattered, still knows.

Whispered Flames in Snow

In the hush, soft embers speak,
Through the chill, warmth they seek.
Snowflakes kiss the silent ground,
As whispered flames dance around.

Softly glowing, hearts align,
Fire's glow in winter's design.
Beneath the frost, a pulse does thrum,
Quiet beats, love's tender drum.

Voices linger, sweet and low,
In the cold, a subtle show.
Wrapped in dreams, we find our way,
Holding tight through night and day.

In every breath, a flicker stays,
Guiding us through snow's embrace.
Flames of passion, whispers blend,
In this chill, love will not end.

So let the world frost over deep,
In whispered flames, our hearts will leap.
Together wrapped in winter's glow,
We find our warmth in falling snow.

Embers in the Arctic Chill

In the frosty land where shadows play,
Embers glow softly, lighting the way.
Whispers of warmth amidst the freeze,
Courage ignites like a gentle breeze.

Stars twinkle brightly in the endless night,
Each flicker a promise, a glimmer of light.
Hearts beat steady beneath winter's embrace,
Finding their rhythm in this sacred space.

Snowflakes dance softly, a delicate waltz,
Nature's pure beauty, without any faults.
While the world slumbers under a white shroud,
Hope stirs within, silent yet proud.

Frostbitten Glimmers

Glimmers of light on frosted grass,
Nature's jewels as moments pass.
Each breath a cloud in the crisp air,
Frostbitten dreams linger everywhere.

Windows glisten with icy lace,
In this chilly world, we find our place.
Stories unfold in the crackling fire,
A warmth ignites, pulling us higher.

Footsteps crunch on a snow-covered path,
Laughing together, we dance and laugh.
Life's precious warmth in winter's embrace,
Frostbitten glimmers that time can't erase.

Icy Whispers of Passion

In the quiet whispers, our secrets reside,
Icy tendrils of longing, we cannot hide.
With every glance, a fire is sparked,
In this frozen world, our love is marked.

Beneath the surface, where hearts intertwine,
Frost gives way to the sweetest design.
Each moment a treasure, a delicate sigh,
In the depths of winter, our spirits will fly.

Fates have conspired, two souls aligned,
In the breath of frost, true love we find.
Beneath the stars, where the cold winds wail,
Icy whispers guide us, an unbroken tale.

Chilled Hearts on Fire

Chilled hearts awaken to the warmth inside,
Through frosty nights, side by side we bide.
Laughter echoes through the crisp night air,
While flickers of passion ignite everywhere.

Wrapped in blankets, our dreams take flight,
In the depth of winter, everything feels right.
Fires burn bright, casting shadows long,
Melodies rise, like a well-loved song.

Embers whisper tales of what's to be,
Chilled hearts on fire, forever we'll be.
In the tapestry woven by our shared spark,
Together, we light every path in the dark.

Icebound Passion

In the hollows where silence reigns,
Frozen hearts clasp in chains.
Chilled breaths beneath the pale moon,
Yearning whispers, a muted tune.

Frosted dreams with shadows drift,
Crystals glimmer, a hidden gift.
In the stillness, desires ignite,
A fire buried within the night.

Glistening tears on ice so clear,
Echoes of love, both far and near.
Yearn to break the cold embrace,
To melt the barriers we face.

Through the storm, our spirits meet,
In a dance that feels so sweet.
Together we brave the frozen lands,
Bound by fate, hand in hand.

Awakening with the dawn's first light,
Hearts unshackled, ready for flight.
Where ice once held, passion shall flow,
In the warmth of love, forever we grow.

Whispers of Lava Under Ice

Beneath the icy crust, a fervor lies,
Molten desires hidden from our eyes.
Silent echoes in the frozen core,
A rumbling heart, longing for more.

Heat pulses under layers of frost,
In this stillness, energy is not lost.
Lava murmurs its secrets deep,
Yearning for freedom, in silence it weeps.

Cracks appear in the shimmering ground,
A dance of elements, life's new sound.
Fire and ice in a delicate play,
Whispers of change in the light of day.

As the thaw begins, bring forth the light,
From the depths, a passionate fight.
Eruption of love, so fierce, so bold,
Embers rise from the stories untold.

In a clash of forces, worlds collide,
Love's raw power cannot be denied.
Beneath this ice, where heat and cold meet,
Lava and whispers in a fiery heartbeat.

Sparkling Frost's Lament

Upon the glassy surface bright,
Frost weaves tales in morning light.
Each crystal holds a story dear,
A whispered sigh, a frozen tear.

Nature's art in delicate scenes,
Sparkling beauty hides shattered dreams.
In the cold, where shadows creep,
Frost laments while the world sleeps.

A tapestry of silvery white,
Veils of sorrow in gentle flight.
Every shimmer speaks of loss,
The burden of the frost's own cross.

Through the winter's bitter breath,
Echoes linger, a dance with death.
But in the dark, hope still glows,
For every ending, a new path grows.

As spring approaches, warmth returns,
Frost melts away, yet still it yearns.
A mingling of life, of joy regained,
In each new bloom, the heart's unchained.

Whispers of Icy Ember

Amidst the chill, embers glow bright,
Icy whispers, a flickering light.
Under the snow, an ardor remains,
Silent warmth in frostbitten veins.

The dance of fire and ice so divine,
Sparks of passion through the cold intertwine.
With soft sighs, the night takes its hold,
Stories of love in the frost unfold.

Frozen trees, like sentinels stand,
Guarding secrets in the winter's hand.
From the ashes, memories gleam,
In the silence, we build our dream.

Through the winters, our hearts stay brave,
For muted embers, no storm can enslave.
In the shadows, love's warmth is clear,
Whispers of hope, forever near.

As spring awakens, embrace the sun,
Embers burn bright, the ice is undone.
From winter's chill, we rise anew,
With whispers of love, ever true.

Snowbound Radiance

In silence deep, the winter glows,
A blanket bright where soft light flows.
Each flake a gem, a whispered vow,
Time stands still beneath the boughs.

Footsteps trace a path of white,
As day transforms into the night.
Stars above like diamonds gleam,
In this cold, we live the dream.

Frosted breath in chilly air,
Moments wrapped in magic rare.
Every sigh a frozen kiss,
In snow's embrace, we find our bliss.

The world is hushed, the heart beats slow,
In winter's dance, we feel the flow.
Radiance shining, pure and bright,
In this boundless, snowy light.

Nature's art on every tree,
A tapestry for all to see.
Each branch adorned with crystal lace,
In snowbound radiance, we find grace.

Ice-Kissed Heat

Amid the chill, a warmth ignites,
Two souls entwined on wintry nights.
A fire burns beneath the frost,
In this duality, none are lost.

Fingers intertwined, we glow,
Ice-kissed heat, where embers flow.
Every glance a heated spark,
As passion glimmers through the dark.

The world outside, a frozen stone,
Yet in this haven, we're not alone.
Hearts collide in the cold's embrace,
Drawing warmth from this sacred space.

We laugh aloud, our breaths like smoke,
In this warmth, we are bespoke.
Ice meets fire, a dance so sweet,
In a world of frost, we find our beat.

Love's light shines, both fierce and true,
In winter's clasp, it's me and you.
With every moment, passion's play,
Ice-kissed heat will never fray.

Searing Serenity

In the stillness, we find our peace,
A whispered breeze, the world's release.
Golden rays through leaves do play,
Searing calm in the light of day.

Moments linger, time stands still,
As nature breathes, we feel the thrill.
Every heartbeat sings a song,
In this serenity, we belong.

Clouds drift softly across the blue,
Painting dreams for me and you.
Serene horizons, wide and free,
In every sight, a jubilee.

The sun dips low, a fiery glow,
With shadows dancing, soft and slow.
In twilight's arms, we find our way,
Searing serenity leads the day.

Together here, our spirits soar,
A tranquil heart that's ever more.
In the warmth of this golden scene,
We find the peace we've always seen.

Frigid Flicker

Beneath the stars, the cold winds sway,
A flicker bright amidst the gray.
Candles glow with gentle light,
Frigid whispers on winter's night.

Each flame a tale, each shadow plays,
In soft refrains, the heart obeys.
A dance of warmth in icy air,
Where hope ignites, we share a prayer.

The world outside is crisp and bright,
But here we bask in firelight.
Frigid nights can't touch our spark,
As laughter echoes through the dark.

Moments captured, flickers freeze,
In winter's arms, we find our ease.
Through frosted panes, the moon does shine,
In frigid flicker, hearts align.

With every breath, the chill recedes,
Within this warmth, our soul proceeds.
Together strong, against the cold,
In frigid flicker, love unfolds.

Shimmering Ice Heart

In the quiet of winter's night,
A heart that glimmers, cold and bright.
Trapped in silence, yet it beats,
Echoing softly, time retreats.

Crystals dance on frosted trees,
Whispers carried by the breeze.
Glistening under the pale moon,
A melody, a frozen tune.

Deep within a frozen lake,
Dreams awaken, softly quake.
Under layers, secrets lie,
Shimmering beneath the sky.

With each heartbeat, cracks appear,
Fragile love, sincere yet clear.
In the depths of icy art,
Lies the warmth of a hidden heart.

As the seasons start to shift,
Nature's hand begins to lift.
The ice may break, yet still will shine,
For within, a love divine.

Ashes Beneath the Ice

Winter covers all in white,
But below, there's hidden light.
Ashes smolder, quiet glow,
Silent stories, deep below.

Cracked surfaces hide the truth,
Whispers of forgotten youth.
Flames once bright, now held in time,
Beneath the layers, lost in rhyme.

Snowflakes touch like soft regret,
Memories of warmth not met.
Every flake, a fleeting dream,
Lost forever, or so it seems.

As the thaw begins to creep,
Awakens dreams from restless sleep.
The ashes stir, a soft embrace,
Beneath the ice, a vibrant trace.

Though frozen now, they hold the fire,
From coldness springs a fierce desire.
Resilient hearts will rise once more,
From ashes deep, new flames will soar.

Flame's Blessing in Winter

Against the chill, embers glow,
A fire's warmth in winter's show.
Each flicker sings a calming song,
A promise that we all belong.

Beneath the snow, the ground will breathe,
Life lies waiting, sure to seethe.
Flame's blessing grants us grace,
In this serene and icy space.

Hands held tight to capture heat,
Through breathless air, our hearts will meet.
Even as the cold winds blow,
Together, we face the winter's woe.

In flickering light, shadows dance,
Casting dreams upon a chance.
Though winter's grasp can feel so long,
With flame's blessing, we grow strong.

As dawn breaks through the frosty gleam,
We weave our wishes into a dream.
In winter's heart, still burns the fire,
Fueling hope and sweet desire.

Radiant Ice

Icicles form like crystal blades,
In the sunlight, beauty wades.
Radiance trapped in frozen streams,
A world alive with frosty dreams.

Every flake, a diamond bright,
A fleeting moment, pure delight.
In the quiet, whispers soar,
As icy fingers scratch the shore.

Beneath the surface, life does hide,
In stillness, creatures glide and bide.
Colorful hues beneath the frost,
In silent realms, nothing is lost.

Vibrant light through snowy trees,
Nature's art, a masterpiece.
In the chill, we find the grace,
Of radiant ice, a sacred space.

As seasons change, the ice will melt,
Yet within, true warmth is felt.
The beauty lies in moments brief,
In radiant ice, we find our peace.

Ember's Winter Song

In the chill of the night,
Embers softly glow bright.
Whispers of warmth and cheer,
Hold the frost deep and near.

Snowflakes dance in the air,
A ballet of winter's stare.
Through the silence they fall,
Nature's soft, tender call.

In the heart of the cold,
Stories of warmth unfold.
Each flame that brightly gleams,
Ignites our deepest dreams.

As shadows shift and sway,
Winter sings its old lay.
With every flicker's rise,
Hope ignites in the skies.

Feel the breath of the breeze,
Crisp and fresh, yet it frees.
In the ember's soft song,
We find where we belong.

Frigid Flickers

By the hearth's glowing light,
Frigid flickers take flight.
Whispers of warmth cascade,
As winter's chill starts to fade.

The crackle fills the room,
Chasing off night's looming gloom.
In the dance of the flame,
Every spark has a name.

Through the windows we see,
A world cold, wild, and free.
Yet inside, hearts ignite,
In the warmth of the night.

Each flicker tells a tale,
Of winter's icy veil.
With cozy blankets near,
We savor the frost's sneer.

Frigid winds howl and bite,
Yet we hold our dreams tight.
In the light, we embrace,
The beauty of this space.

Heart of Ice

In the stillness of night,
A heart trapped in pure white.
Veins of ice run so deep,
Secrets in shadows keep.

Winter's grip holds so fast,
Memories drift to the past.
Yet beneath rigid seams,
Lies the flutter of dreams.

Frozen tears mark the ground,
In silence, they gather 'round.
But hope's fire still hums,
When the springtime heart comes.

Though the chill may confine,
Even ice can align.
In the thaw's tender kiss,
Find the warmth that you miss.

Time will melt all the strife,
Breathing life into life.
From the heart of the ice,
Emerges a love so nice.

Kindled Snow

Snowflakes drift from above,
Whispers of winter's love.
Together they twirl and spin,
In each flake, we begin.

Crisp air fills the night sky,
As soft footprints comply.
In this blanket of white,
Dreams take flight, pure and bright.

Every flake tells a tale,
Fragments of frost that sail.
In the quiet we find,
A kindled spark intertwined.

Through the frozen embrace,
Heartbeats quicken their pace.
A moment shared in glow,
Underneath kindled snow.

In the hush, warmth ignites,
Through the cold, we find lights.
Together, hand in hand,
In this wintery land.

Fiery Chill

In shadows deep where embers glow,
A paradox in breezes blow.
The warmth of flame in winter's grasp,
A dance of light, a cold reprieve.

Fiery Chill

Crisp is the air, yet hearts ignite,
With every spark, the stars alight.
A warmth that flickers, never dead,
In icy winds, the passion spread.

Fiery Chill

Crackling whispers, secrets shared,
Melting ice with flames prepared.
A chill that bites, yet draws us near,
In fiery chill, we lose our fear.

Fiery Chill

Embers pulse in frozen nights,
Guiding souls to love's delights.
Through chilly veils of mist and flame,
In fiery chill, we're not the same.

Fiery Chill

A journey bold through darkened pine,
With hearts entwined, your hand in mine.
Though winter's chill may freeze our breath,
In fiery chill, we conquer death.

Fiery Chill

Unraveled tales where echoes meet,
In twilight's grasp, the hearts compete.
For warmth persists despite the chill,
Our fiery love, a constant thrill.

Mystic Frostfire

Whispers of frost wrapped 'round the flame,
Mirrored reflections, untamed names.
In silent woods where shadows weep,
The frost and fire their secrets keep.

Mystic Frostfire

A hallowed ground where spirits play,
With frosty fingers guiding sway.
The flames are dancing, shadows twirling,
In mystic realms, the worlds unfurling.

Mystic Frostfire

Textures woven with chill and heat,
In every touch, our destinies meet.
Through flickering lights of joy and tears,
We find the magic that transcends years.

Mystic Frostfire

Skies of twilight, a perfect blend,
Where frost meets fire, beginnings mend.
A tapestry of vibrant glow,
In mystic frostfire, love will flow.

Mystic Frostfire

Echoes of laughter, hearts that soar,
In every heartbeat, we find more.
An alchemy of night and day,
In frostfire's grip, we drift away.

Harbored warm whispers

In hidden glades where time stands still,
Soft as a dream, a gentle thrill.
Whispers carried on the breeze,
Wrapped in warmth, the heart's unease.

Harbored warm whispers

Secrets shared beneath the stars,
In hushed tones, we mend the scars.
Each soft breath, a promise made,
In tender moments, fears will fade.

Harbored warm whispers

Through tangled branches, light will stream,
Finding solace in the dream.
Two souls connected, hearts entwined,
In sacred hush, pure love we find.

Harbored warm whispers

The echoes dance on moonlit streams,
Cradled softly in our dreams.
With every glance, the world unknown,
In warm whispers, we have grown.

Harbored warm whispers

In cozy corners, hands held tight,
We share our hopes beneath the night.
A sanctuary where love reigns,
In whispered tones, deep joy remains.

Fire's Lament in the Frost

In winter's grip, the embers sigh,
A haunting song of days gone by.
The flames once bright now flicker low,
In frost's embrace, their warmth does stow.

Fire's Lament in the Frost

Each crackle tells of warmth and glow,
Stories of fire we used to know.
Yet frost brings forth a chilling breath,
In each lament lies echoes of death.

Fire's Lament in the Frost

A dance of shadows, flickers fight,
In quiet nights, a fading light.
The fire's voice a soft refrain,
Whispers lost in winter's pain.

Fire's Lament in the Frost

In frozen fields where ashes lie,
The spirit speaks, the embers cry.
For every flame that dared to leap,
In frost's lament, the fire sleeps.

Fire's Lament in the Frost

Yet every dusk brings forth a dawn,
And from the cold, new life is drawn.
With hope reborn, the shadows yield,
In fire's lament, a warmth revealed.

Fire's Lament in the Frost

So we remain, both cold and bright,
The fire's sorrow, a guiding light.
In frosty nights, the embers glow,
A timeless tale, in whispers flow.

Glacial Glow

In the silence of the night,
A pale light starts to gleam,
Dancing on the icy hill,
Whispering a frosty dream.

Shadows play on silver ice,
Nature's breath is crisp and light,
Crystals form like frozen lace,
Underneath the starry sight.

Glacial rivers flow with grace,
Reflecting hues of twilight,
Every movement soft and slow,
In a world wrapped up so tight.

Echoes of the calm and cold,
Store whispers of the day's delight,
In the diamond-studded air,
Where winter weaves her magic bright.

As the dawn begins to rise,
Shimmering in soft pink hues,
Glacial glow begins to fade,
Leaving magic in its muse.

Ember Frost

The fire crackles, sparks will fly,
Yet frost nips at my toes,
In the hearth's warm embrace,
A gentle tension grows.

Embers dance, a fleeting light,
While chill seeps through the door,
Each breath shows the battle fought,
Heartfelt warmth craving more.

Veils of warmth, they whisper low,
Desires twinkle and ignite,
A paradox of frozen breath,
In a realm of day and night.

Paths of warmth and frost collide,
Leaving trails both sharp and sweet,
Moments shared in a fleeting gaze,
As fire and frost entwine their beat.

In the twilight glow we meet,
Shadows cast by flick'ring bliss,
Every touch ignites a spark,
In this icy world, a warm kiss.

Shivers of Desire

Underneath a pale moon's light,
Whispers float upon the breeze,
Chilled by air so crisp and bright,
A heart quakes with hopes and pleas.

Desires linger, soft and sweet,
In the frost-clad, silent night,
Yearning eyes that dare to meet,
Shivers warmth and cold unite.

Each breath mingles in the air,
Promises wrapped in silver haze,
Cool caress, igniting fires,
In this dance of magic plays.

With every heartbeat, shadows sway,
Echoes of a silent song,
Moments pause, as dreams convey,
Entwined, where both belong.

Eyes that glimmer, hearts that race,
In the chill of winter's grasp,
Fleeting moments, tender space,
Holding on, when love's a gasp.

Cold Radiance

A shimmer in the frozen dawn,
Where shadows slide in icy breath,
Cold radiance gently drawn,
Life and beauty dance with death.

Amidst the silent, snowy fields,
Crystalline sparks light the sky,
Nature's beauty softly yields,
To the touch of passing by.

Glints of silver flicker bright,
As the world slows down its pace,
Frosty edges catch the light,
In this quiet, sacred space.

Whispers travel on the wind,
Tales of wishes yet to come,
Hearts united, lost, and pinned,
Underneath the chill's soft drum.

Cold radiance, a fleeting glow,
Brushes softly, pure and bright,
In the gaze of softest snow,
Where love meets the morning light.

Pyres in the Snow

In winter's chill, the flames arise,
They dance like spirits in the skies.
A warmth ignites the frozen land,
As shadows flicker, bold and grand.

Embers glow, through white they roam,
A heartbeat finds its fleeting home.
Through swirling winds, the sparks will fly,
As cold retreats, and echoes die.

The pyres burn with stories old,
Of battles fought and legends told.
In every spark, a memory glows,
As winter's breath begins to slow.

In silence deep, the night is sewn,
Beneath the stars, this warmth is grown.
In harmony, the fire's light,
Defies the long and frigid night.

So in the snow, let warmth take hold,
Where memories burn, fierce and bold.
With every flicker, dreams will rise,
Pyres in the snow, beneath the skies.

Petals of Ice

Amidst the frost, soft petals fall,
Delicate whispers that enthrall.
Each crystal bloom, a fleeting grace,
In winter's grasp, a hidden place.

They shimmer bright, a fragile art,
A beauty held within the heart.
In gardens cold, their colors reign,
Emerging bright from winter's bane.

With each descent, a story spun,
Of fleeting time and battles won.
In icy frames, their spirits soar,
Petals of ice forever more.

The world transforms, a canvas white,
Where dreams are etched in bold delight.
Among the chill, their warmth will bloom,
In frozen fields, abolishing gloom.

So let us dance where frost will weave,
A tapestry, we will believe.
With every step, the petals sigh,
In harmony with the winter sky.

Defiant Heat

In sweltering days, the sun will blaze,
A fiery dance in summer's haze.
With every breath, the spirit gleams,
In focus found within our dreams.

The heat defies, a willful force,
Through sweat and toil, we find our course.
As shadows stretch, a tale unfolds,
Of courage fierce, of hearts so bold.

With every spark, we rise anew,
A warmth that pulses deep and true.
In restless nights, the heat ignites,
Defiant hearts reaching new heights.

In blazing fields, the colors sing,
A symphony of the joys we bring.
We face the fire, embrace the glow,
In every moment, we learn and grow.

So through the heat, we stand as one,
Embracing warmth, until we're done.
In every beat, our spirits rise,
Defiant heat beneath the skies.

Frost's Silent Embrace

In twilight's grip, the frost descends,
A silent touch that slowly bends.
With whispered breath, it cloaks the night,
In icy veils of silver light.

The world stands still, a canvas bare,
With every crystal, beauty's flare.
In frosted breath, the dreams awake,
A quiet lull, a tender ache.

Each edge is sharp, each line defined,
In perfect form, the world aligned.
Through winter's grasp, we find our peace,
In frozen moments, time will cease.

In shadows deep, the magic plays,
As frost transforms the long, cold days.
In silent spaces, warmth can grow,
Amidst the chill, our hearts can glow.

So let us dwell in frost's embrace,
Finding solace in every place.
In tranquil nights, where dreams will race,
We'll find our hope in winter's grace.

Whirlwind of Frost

A dance of snowflakes spirals down,
Whispers of chill in a twilight gown.
Trees shiver under a diamond sheet,
Nature's breath, a frosty treat.

Icicles hung like crystal knives,
In silence, the winter thrives.
The world transformed, pure and white,
Each moment frozen, day turned night.

Footsteps crunch on the powdered ground,
Memories linger without a sound.
The air so crisp, a sharp refrain,
Laughter echoes in winter's lane.

A whirlwind spins, a tempest's play,
Chasing the warmth of a sunlit ray.
In this magic, the heart feels bold,
Wrapped in stories long foretold.

Embrace the frost, embrace the chill,
For in this beauty, time stands still.
A whirlwind of frost, a fleeting dream,
In winter's arms, we wander, we gleam.

Consumed by Winter's Breath

Cold winds whisper through the trees,
Breath of winter upon the breeze.
Shadows stretch across the white,
Day descends into quiet night.

Fireplaces crackle with warmth,
While outside, the snowflakes swarm.
The world wears white, a tranquil dress,
In the stillness, a soft caress.

Branches bow beneath the weight,
Nature's hush, a solemn state.
Stars emerge in a velvet sky,
As frozen dreams begin to sigh.

The moon casts light on fields of frost,
A beauty gained but warmth is lost.
Consumed by winter's tranquil breath,
Life slows down, in quiet death.

Each flake a memory, soft and light,
In shadows deep, we find our night.
Tender moments, fleeting and rare,
In winter's grasp, we breathe the air.

Vanish Embers

A flicker fades in the hearth's embrace,
As shadows dance in the lonely space.
Whispers of warmth begin to wane,
Leaving behind a ghost of flame.

The firelight dims, a soft retreat,
Leaving behind the echo of heat.
In the ashes, memories burn,
A flickering light where we yearn.

Outside, the chill wraps heart and soul,
Once vibrant embers now take their toll.
Night settles in with a quiet sigh,
As gray clouds blanket the dusky sky.

Voices linger in the fading light,
Tales of warmth through the velvet night.
But as the embers vanish away,
We cling to memories that choose to stay.

In silence, the charcoal turns to dust,
While dreams still shimmer, as they must.
Vanish embers, like whispers lost,
Yet we hold tight, no matter the cost.

Kindling Amidst Frost

In the heart of winter's embrace,
Kindling glows, a sacred space.
Amongst the frost, a spark ignites,
Filling the dark with hopeful lights.

Branches bare against the sky,
Yet within, warm embers lie.
A promise whispered through the chill,
To face the cold, to seek the thrill.

Snowflakes fall, a soft ballet,
Covering dreams in their gentle sway.
Yet beneath the frost, life stirs anew,
Awakening visions that shine through.

The kindling cracks with a tender sound,
Resilience found in the frozen ground.
Each flicker dances, a silent cheer,
Amongst life's trials, winter's near.

So gather close, let warmth surround,
In the heart of frost, hope can be found.
Kindling amidst the winter's breath,
A fire of life, defying death.

Resilient Heat

In the heart of winter's chill,
A flame ignites our will.
Against the frost it stands strong,
A whisper of warmth in the throng.

Through the storm, we find our way,
With hope that light won't sway.
Each ember glows, a distant star,
Reminding us just how far.

Beneath the snowfall, dreams awake,
In every choice that we make.
Fortitude like iron binds,
Giving strength to weary minds.

Even as the shadows creep,
Our spirit wakes from sleep.
Resilience fuels the fire,
Carving paths that never tire.

So let the cold winds blow,
We'll nurture what we know.
With kindred souls nearby,
We'll rise, we'll never die.

Bright Within the Snow

In blankets white, the world does pause,
Yet hidden light within the jaws.
Each flake a gem, a tale untold,
Of warmth and laughter, brave and bold.

As sunlight dances on the ice,
A glimmering of sweet device.
The crisp air holds a promise clear,
Of springtime's joy that draws us near.

Footsteps crunch beneath our haste,
Moments treasured, never waste.
Bright smiles flicker like the stars,
Painted dreams that heal our scars.

The chill may bite, but hearts are warm,
In this white wonderland, a charm.
With every breath, together we flow,
Creating magic in the snow.

So gather close, let's share this grace,
In frosty fields, our sacred space.
For bright within this quiet glow,
Lies love that nurtures seeds to grow.

Silent Firelight

In the stillness of the night,
Dancing shadows, flickers bright.
The fire whispers tales of yore,
Of passion, loss, and dreams in store.

Embers crackle with old wounds,
Healing time, in softened tunes.
A warmth that wraps around the soul,
In silent moments, we feel whole.

The darkness holds a secret tight,
Within the glow, we find our light.
Each spark a memory that glows,
Of love, of laughter, and the prose.

As flames leap high with gentle grace,
We gather close, embrace our space.
In unity, our hearts ignite,
A bond unbroken through the night.

Let the world outside remain,
For here we shed our every pain.
In silent firelight, we reside,
With hearts as one, forever tied.

Cold Breath of Desire

In winter's breath, the longing stirs,
A quiet ache that softly purrs.
Frigid air wraps close around,
In every heart, a flame is found.

Desire blooms beneath the frost,
In silent whispers, lines embossed.
A promise made in every sigh,
As dreams of warmth begin to fly.

The chill may penetrate the skin,
Yet sparks of passion dwell within.
In frozen hush, connection grows,
A river of longing gently flows.

Embracing cold, we find our fire,
In shared moments, we conspire.
Through lonely nights, we dare to hope,
In the depths of frost, we learn to cope.

So let the world in white unfold,
In the heart, a warmth to hold.
For in each breath that stirs the air,
Desire lives, a love laid bare.

Veiled Flames in the Winter

In silence cold, the embers glow,
Wrapped in blankets of the snow.
Whispers dance with frosty breath,
Each flame a tale of warmth and death.

The moonlight casts on frozen ground,
While flickers of the heart resound.
Beneath the chill, the spirit plays,
Ember's light, a fiery gaze.

Veils of white, with red exposed,
The winter's chill, yet heart's enclosed.
Each bond ignites in glimmers bright,
Amidst the darkness, there's still light.

As shadows lengthen with the dusk,
The world feels hushed, embraced in musk.
When winds arise, will we still find,
The warmth that lingers in our mind?

To hold through storms, enduring fate,
With veiled flames, our hope's innate.
Together standing, brave and bold,
In winter's grasp, our love is told.

Frosted Whimsy

In morning light, the world aglow,
A frosted whimsy, soft and slow.
Each glitter flake, a dance so rare,
Sprinkled dreams float through the air.

Glistening trails on silent eaves,
Nature's quilt beneath the leaves.
Childlike laughter fills the space,
As snowflakes fall, they weave a grace.

Magic whispers in playful winds,
Where every joy and moment spins.
In winter's clutch, the heart can sing,
Frosted whimsy, a gentle ring.

As shadows stretch, the day fades out,
Still, warmth remains, without a doubt.
In cozy corners, stories blend,
As frosted dreams shall never end.

So here we stand, together, free,
In whimsy's grasp, just you and me.
Where frosted laughter never tires,
In winter's glow, our hearts are fires.

Intangible Heat

In shadowed rooms where whispers soar,
An intangible heat, forevermore.
Beneath the chill, a pulsing glow,
A tether strong, though unseen flow.

When time stands still, the world asleep,
We hold the warmth that we can keep.
In secret glances, fingers trace,
The longing found in each embrace.

Outside, the frost paints stories bright,
While inside burns a soft, warm light.
In every moment, every sigh,
Intangible heat, we can't deny.

Amidst the cold, our spirits leap,
In whispered dreams, it's ours to reap.
The fire within, it softly hums,
A silent song that always comes.

So let the winter wind rush by,
In heated hearts, love never lies.
We'll forge a path through the snows afar,
Chasing warmth, wherever you are.

Shrouded Ember

Amidst the twilight's gentle mist,
A shrouded ember, cannot resist.
It flickers low, yet holds its trust,
In quiet spaces, strong and just.

The world may fade in dusky hues,
But in the dark, the heart renews.
Each pulse a whisper, a secret bold,
In silence vast, it's love retold.

Through shadowed paths, where echoes play,
The ember glows, as night gives way.
With every breath, a warmth we spark,
In shadows deep, igniting dark.

Where winter winds may chill the bone,
A shrouded ember feels at home.
In every glance, a promise laid,
In mutual warmth, we won't be swayed.

So let the fire simmer slow,
In hidden depths, love's quiet flow.
Shrouded embers, we'll always find,
In heart's embrace, forever bind.

Crystal Blaze

In the heart of the night, so bright,
Shimmers of stars dance in flight.
A glow that sets the ice aglow,
Whispers of warmth in the winter's flow.

Sparkling dreams paint the cold air,
Each flake a secret, beyond compare.
Flickering flames, a tender embrace,
In the cold, we find our place.

Frosty breath in the moonlit gleam,
Echoes of laughter, a shared dream.
Let the nights be filled with light,
In the blaze of crystals, we take flight.

Softly the winds carry our song,
A melody sweet, where we belong.
Among the shards of frozen light,
Together we'll dance till morning's sight.

So let the crystal blaze unfold,
With stories of warmth forever told.
In the arms of winter we will stay,
A glow of brilliance in the fray.

Silence of the Hearth

In the stillness deep and wide,
The hearth glows with a gentle pride.
Whispers of flames, an age-old tale,
Tales of joy that cannot pale.

Crackling logs in the cozy night,
A refuge found in the fading light.
Hearts warm as shadows dance near,
In the silence, love feels clear.

Each flame a story, a cherished dream,
In the silence, we hear the theme.
Wrapped in warmth and tender grace,
In the hearth's embrace, we find our place.

Outside the chill, a world unknown,
Inside, the fire has brightly grown.
Moments shared, the laughter flows,
In the silence, our spirit glows.

So let us sit by the warming fire,
In the silence, souls inspired.
Gathered close, we'll welcome the night,
In the silence of the hearth, we take flight.

Frozen Radiance

The world is wrapped in a crystal skin,
Radiance found where dreams begin.
Each branch adorned with icy lace,
In frozen beauty, we find grace.

Snowflakes twirl in the gentle breeze,
Nature's dance, a sight to please.
In the stillness, time stands still,
Captured moments that hearts can feel.

Glistening paths through woodland trails,
Echoes of laughter in winter gales.
With every step, the magic glows,
In frozen radiance, happiness shows.

A world reborn in glimmering white,
The sun shines down, a warming light.
In this enchantment, hearts collide,
In the frozen radiance, we abide.

So let us wander where wonders freeze,
And capture joy in the winter's tease.
With every glance, let spirits rise,
In this frozen radiance, our love flies.

Winter's Warmth

In the chill of a winter's night,
We gather close, hearts alight.
A blanket snug, a shared embrace,
In winter's warmth, we find our space.

Ice crystals form on the windowpane,
As laughter dances like gentle rain.
With mugs of cocoa, stories unfold,
In the warmth, we break the cold.

The world outside, a shimmering veil,
While inside, joy tells its tale.
Through frosted glass, the moon does peek,
In winter's warmth, we hear hearts speak.

Candles flicker, casting soft glow,
A haven created, love's gentle flow.
As seasons shift and time will wane,
In winter's warmth, we feel no pain.

So let us cherish these moments tight,
Hold each other through the night.
In the embrace of frost, we'll stay,
Forever warmed by love's array.

Dancing Shadows in Ice

In the silence of the night,
Shadows twirl, a graceful sight.
They glide over frozen streams,
Whispering softly of winter dreams.

Frosted branches sway and bend,
As the dance begins to blend.
Moonlight casts its silver glow,
On a world wrapped in snow.

Underneath the cold expanse,
Nature holds a secret dance.
Echoes of laughter, soft and clear,
Flow through the air, drawing near.

Each step traced in icy blue,
Crafting magic, fresh and new.
In the chill, warmth softly breathes,
Carried on the winter's leaves.

A waltz of shadows, bold and bright,
In the depths of the starry night.
Together, in this chill embrace,
They weave the fabric of time and space.

Firelight in a Frosted Cage

Within the frost, a fire glows,
Casting warmth while the cool wind blows.
Dancing flames, a vibrant hue,
Flicker stories old and new.

The cage of ice begins to melt,
As whispers of heat are gently felt.
Crackling sounds, a soothing balm,
In the heart of winter's calm.

Flames leap high, shadows twist,
Painting dreams that can't be missed.
Trapped within a world so cold,
Yet the fire burns bright and bold.

Around the blaze, spirits gather near,
Sharing tales both far and dear.
In the frost, a lively feast,
Where warmth and joy are shared, at least.

With every spark, hope takes flight,
Defying darkness with its light.
In the heart of winter's snare,
Firelight dances without care.

Glinting Frost

On the grass, a sparkling sheen,
Jewels of winter, bright and keen.
Morning sun sings a soft refrain,
As frost glints gently on the plain.

Each crystal shines in pristine grace,
Nature's art, a pure embrace.
A frosty breath upon the air,
Whispers secrets, soft and rare.

Along the branches, frosted lace,
Delicate patterns, time can't erase.
Silent beauty, cold yet warm,
Hiding life within the storm.

Steps leave prints on winter's ground,
In each corner, magic found.
A world awash in diamond light,
Turns the mundane into delight.

As day unfolds, the frost will fade,
Yet its memory won't be swayed.
In the heart, a lingering glow,
Of glinting frost and morning's show.

The Heat Inside the Chills

Amidst the cold, a fire burns bright,
Creating warmth within the night.
A heartbeat thumps beneath the snow,
Where hidden passions start to flow.

Winter's grasp clings tight and strong,
But within us, we belong.
Through icy winds and frozen streams,
We ignite the spark of dreams.

Fireside flickers tell our tale,
Through hardships, we shall prevail.
With every chill comes a fierce defy,
In the heat inside, we learn to fly.

Hearts ablaze with warm desire,
Burning deeply with each fire.
Even when the world is cold,
We gather strength, the brave and bold.

Together we endure the freeze,
Finding warmth in friendships, ease.
In shadows cast by winter's breath,
We find the heat that conquers death.

So let the winter winds blow strong,
Within our hearts, we will belong.
In the chill, our spirits rise,
Fueled by warmth, we reach the skies.

Teardrops of Melting Heat

Under the sun, the ice does weep,
A tale of warmth in silence deep.
Each teardrop falls with whispered pain,
Reflecting joy, yet marred by stain.

In gardens green where shadows fade,
The molten rays do softly wade.
A dance of sighs in twilight's glow,
As nature shifts, the heat will flow.

The golden beams do gently kiss,
While all must find a fleeting bliss.
Through every drop, a story starts,
The sun ignites our fragile hearts.

When evening comes, the warmth will roam,
In every pocket, seeking home.
The teardrops fall, yet hope survives,
In melting heat, our passion thrives.

So let the sun's embrace be sweet,
In every tear, a world complete.
For in this heat, both loss and gain,
We find our love, through joy and pain.

Frosted Flame Dance

In winter's grip, the flame does sway,
A frosted dance at end of day.
With every flicker, stories told,
Of heat and heart in shimmer bold.

The chill outside, a soft embrace,
While warmth inside lights up the space.
Together they twine, in sweet romance,
A play of shadows, a fiery dance.

As embers glow through frosty nights,
The world outside in silver bites.
Yet here we stand, in warmth and cheer,
The flames protect us, drawing near.

Each spark a promise, each crackle bright,
In frosty whispers, our hearts take flight.
The fire sways, and so do we,
As frost and flame bring harmony.

So let us dance till morning's light,
In frosted flame, we'll hold on tight.
For in this paradox we find,
A love that's free, yet so entwined.

Eternal Chill of Ember

In shadows deep, the ember glows,
A silent pulse where warmth still flows.
Eternal chill, yet fire remains,
In every breath, our heartbeat gains.

Through darkest nights, the whispers crawl,
Of frozen winds that beckon all.
Each flickering light, a fleeting chance,
To feel the chill, to dream, to dance.

The ice may cling, but hope is bright,
In every ember, a flicker of light.
With winter's grasp, our spirits rise,
Together we soar, beneath the skies.

As night turns deep, the stars awake,
In chilling moments, hearts don't break.
For within the cold, there lies a fire,
An eternal chill that lifts us higher.

So hold on tight, when shadows creep,
Within the chill, our dreams we keep.
Embers spark in endless night,
In eternal chill, we find our light.

Wilderness of Light and Ice

In wilderness where shadows blend,
The light and ice begin to mend.
A silent echo of nature's grace,
In every corner, a sacred space.

The frost upon the branches shines,
While sunlight weaves through ancient pines.
A harmony where chaos sleeps,
In frozen depths, the world still peeps.

Snowflakes dance on whispering winds,
While sunlight warms, the day rescinds.
The ice reflects a golden hue,
A wilderness where all feels new.

In quiet moments, time grows still,
The pulse of nature, strong and real.
With every step, a symphony,
Of light and ice—eternity.

So venture forth, let spirits roam,
In wilderness of light, we find our home.
For in this place of stark delight,
We live, we love, in day and night.

Ice-bound Cravings

In winter's grasp, my heart does yearn,
For warmth that flickers, for fires that burn.
The chill wraps close, a frozen shroud,
Yet deep inside, my dreams are loud.

A cup of cocoa, sweet and rich,
A hearth to gather, a cozy niche.
The echoes of laughter fill the air,
Ice-bound cravings, too strong to bear.

Under starlit skies, the world is still,
Yet here I sit, my heart is filled.
With wishes sent on icy winds,
For warmth from love that never ends.

Outside, the frost paints every tree,
But in my soul, it's summer's glee.
I hear the call of firelight's glow,
In ice-bound dreams, my heart will grow.

So let the winter storm do its worst,
Within this warmth, I'll take my thirst.
For ice-bound cravings bring forth light,
A beacon bright in the darkest night.

Candles in the Blizzard

Candles flicker against the storm,
A dance of shadows, a shifting form.
Through blizzard's might, they steadfast stand,
A soft embrace, a guiding hand.

The outside world is wild and white,
Yet here within, a gentle light.
The whispers of warmth fill the air,
As snowflakes swirl without a care.

Each candle holds a tale untold,
Of moments cherished, memories bold.
In quiet corners, their glow ignites,
A refuge found on winter nights.

The window frost, a crystal frame,
As nature carves, the night untame.
But in this room, love's flame resides,
As candles in the blizzard, hope abides.

Together we gather, hearts aligned,
In candlelight, our lives entwined.
Let winds howl fierce, let snowbanks rise,
With candles bright, we touch the skies.

Flames Behind Glass

Behind the glass, the flames do dance,
A shimmering glow, a warm romance.
Outside the storm, the world asleep,
In here, the fire's promise, deep.

Each flicker tells of tales we've shared,
Of laughter, dreams, and love declared.
The warmth surrounding our weary souls,
As time stands still, our hearts enfold.

The crackling wood, a soothing sound,
While icy winds whirl furious around.
But here inside, a refuge made,
Behind the glass, our fears will fade.

As night falls gently, the stars appear,
With whispers of wishes for those held dear.
The flames behind glass bring hope to stay,
In every moment, come what may.

So let the winter rage and roar,
In this cozy nook, we'll love and soar.
For flames behind glass will always shine,
A testament to love divine.

Frozen Sparks

In the stillness, whispers flow,
Through frozen air, where cold winds blow.
Yet in the silence, sparks ignite,
A flicker bold against the night.

Beneath the frost, the embers glow,
A promise kept, though skies are low.
With every breath and every sigh,
We kindle warmth that will not die.

Together we brave the winter's chill,
In frozen sparks, our hearts do fill.
With hopes aflame, we dare to dream,
That love will flourish, like a stream.

So let the cold wind blow its tunes,
And blanket us with silver moons.
For in our hearts, a fire grows,
In frozen sparks, forever glows.

As shadows dance and night descends,
The world outside, where silence blends.
But in our bubble, joy cascades,
With frozen sparks, the darkness fades.

Light in a Winter's Night

In the hush of evening glow,
Stars begin their gentle show.
Moonlight dances on the snow,
Whispers of the night do flow.

Flickers warm from cabins near,
Softly calling, drawing near.
Windows framed in icy lace,
Invite us to a cozy place.

Silent woods, a blanket white,
Shimmering with soft starlight.
Footsteps crunch on frozen ground,
Nature's peacefulness profound.

Breathe in deep, the crisp, cool air,
Magic lingers everywhere.
In the winter's calm embrace,
Find a still and timeless space.

Hope ignites the chilly night,
Hearts aglow in soft twilight.
Though the winter winds may bite,
We'll hold close this lovely light.

Ashes Beneath the Frost

Beneath the snow, the embers lie,
Whispers of a flame gone by.
Memories of warmth and cheer,
Now just shadows, drawing near.

Frozen ground, a silent grave,
Hopes and dreams, the heart did save.
Yet as seasons come and go,
Life will stir beneath the snow.

Little sparks of life will wake,
Through the frost, the earth will shake.
Ashes turn to fertile ground,
In the quiet, life is found.

Frosty breath of winter's chill,
Holds the past, but not its will.
Strength arises, soft and slow,
From the ashes, life will grow.

Hold your heart and keep it close,
In the dark, it is the most.
For beneath the winter's veil,
Every ending births a tale.

Radiant Chill

A crystal world, so clear and bright,
Underneath the pale moonlight.
Breath of winter fills the air,
Radiance beyond compare.

Ice-encrusted branches sway,
Nature's beauty on display.
Every flake a work of art,
Crafted by a gentle heart.

Whispers carried by the breeze,
Echo softly through the trees.
Every shadow, every light,
Wraps the world in pure delight.

Cold and warm, they intertwine,
Every moment, simply divine.
Let your spirit take its flight,
In this realm of radiant light.

As the dusk begins to fade,
Find your peace in twilight's shade.
In the chill, a warmth you'll feel,
Truth and beauty, oh so real.

Cold Pyre

Fires burn with embers cold,
Stories of the brave and bold.
Crackling wood and fading heat,
Moments lost, a bittersweet.

December winds, they howl and cry,
Masked in shadows, spirits fly.
Echoes haunt the winter night,
Remnants of a once-held light.

Gathered round the dying flame,
Whispers soft, but none the same.
Tales of warmth bring tears anew,
As the cold bids us adieu.

In the ashes, dreams take flight,
Fleeting memories, dimmed by night.
Still we hold what once was bright,
In the heart, a spark ignites.

From the pyre, new hope will rise,
In the darkness, love never dies.
Though the chill may touch the bone,
In memory, we're not alone.

Searing Stillness

In the hush of noon, time stands still,
Beneath the sun's hot, relentless spill.
The heat ripples, a shimmering mirage,
Silence wraps the earth, a solemn barrage.

Sweat beads on brows, the air thick as tar,
A lonely breeze whispers from afar.
Nature holds its breath, a pause in the day,
In this searing stillness, thoughts drift away.

Shadows stretch long, the landscape turns gold,
In the simmering silence, secrets unfold.
The world seems to pause, caught in that trance,
Embracing the heat, lost in the dance.

Then twilight arrives with a gentle sigh,
Washing away the heat, as colors comply.
Stars blink awake, in the cool of the night,
Searing stillness fades, embracing the light.

Under the vast and velveted dome,
We find solace here, a place to roam.
In the warmth of the day, the stillness remains,
In the heart of the heat, life's rhythm sustains.

Gleam Under the Ice

Beneath the frost, the earth lies in dreams,
A world encased in glistening beams.
Each flake a whisper, soft and refined,
In the chill, hidden treasures entwined.

The rivers are quiet, secrets they keep,
Encased in a blanket, lulled into sleep.
Yet, under the surface, a spark still glows,
A pulse of life where the cold wind blows.

Ice crystals shimmer, a delicate lace,
Reflecting the light with an elegant grace.
In the still of the winter, magic resides,
A gleam under the ice where beauty abides.

Footsteps are muffled on snow-cloaked trails,
Nature's soft encore, in whispers, it sails.
The world feels suspended in frosty delight,
As time dances slowly, veiled in pure white.

Yet, beneath it all, the warmth will return,
A promise of spring, in hearts we discern.
For a gleam under ice is but a refrain,
In cycles of nature, life's sweet refrain.

Dance of the Frostbound

In the coldest hour, shadows arise,
Figures move slowly 'neath weeping skies.
A melody lingers, haunting and light,
Guided by whispers of winter's invite.

Step by step in the glistening snow,
Embrace the chill, let the rhythm flow.
Each movement a story, told by the frost,
In a dance intertwined, nothing is lost.

Laughter like crystal, ringing through trees,
Carried on breezes, a sigh in the freeze.
The night holds its breath, as twinkling stars,
Join in the movement, erasing our scars.

Under the moon, the frostbound take flight,
Embodying dreams in the sharpness of night.
They spin and they sway, with grace and with glee,
In the dance of the frostbound, wild and free.

Though soon the dawn will banish the dark,
And warm light will quell this beautiful spark,
In memory's echo, forever they'll roam,
The dance of the frostbound, calling us home.

Glacial Spark

Amid icy valleys, silence prevails,
Whispers of nature weave intricate trails.
A glacial spark ignites in the chill,
Flickering softly, bending time to its will.

Crystals of winter, they shimmer and shine,
Captured reflections, a beautiful sign.
Within the stillness, a heartbeat is found,
In this frozen canvas, life does abound.

Echoes of age, in the frostbitten air,
Tell stories of mountains, majestic and rare.
The sun's gentle touch, melting fears to embers,
Brings warmth to the heart, a fire it remembers.

As sun breaks the dawn, shadows start to flee,
Releasing the grip of winter's decree.
Each glacial spark, a promise, a light,
Whispers of dawn chasing away the night.

Through seasons that change, through trials we face,
In every glimmer, find beauty and grace.
For in icy embrace, beneath winter's arc,
Lies hope everlasting, the glacial spark.

Pyrotechnic Ice

Frosty sparks in twilight glow,
Dancing flames in winter's flow.
Colors clash in silent night,
Beauty blooms, a cold delight.

Glittering shards, a crystal dance,
Underneath the moon's soft glance.
Each flicker, a frozen wisp,
Boundless wonder, a fleeting lisp.

Echoes whisper through the chill,
As time lingers, yet stands still.
Fire and frost, a sweet embrace,
In this realm, a wondrous space.

Chasing dreams on icy trails,
In this land where magic sails.
Every spark, a story told,
Laced in silver, rimmed in gold.

Through the night, the colors play,
In a world of hues, they sway.
Pyrotechnic ice, a marvel bright,
Holding time in frozen light.

Subzero Inferno

Amidst the frost, a fire burns,
In frigid winds, the passion churns.
Embers glow in icy air,
Opposites meet, a wild affair.

Blazing hearts in winter's clutch,
Every spark ignites the hush.
Frosted flames begin to dance,
Lost in a fervent, frozen trance.

Flames that flicker, bright and low,
In the icy breeze, they glow.
Heat and cold, a daring song,
In this realm where both belong.

Underneath the starry dome,
Find your way, feel right at home.
Subzero inferno's fierce embrace,
In its grip, we find our place.

In the still, the warmth ignites,
Chasing shadows, chasing sights.
Weaving stories in the night,
Of love aflame and pure delight.

Ashen Serenity

Grey as clouds that softly drift,
In the silence, our spirits lift.
Softly falls the gentle ash,
Memories in the quiet clash.

Stillness wraps the world tonight,
An embrace of muted light.
Amidst the flames that once roared high,
Calm descends, and embers die.

A whispering breeze, a tender sigh,
Nature's peace, as time slips by.
In the ashen layers deep,
Sleep is woven in the heap.

Roots hold fast beneath the grey,
Grounded in the twilight's stay.
Through the still, a gentle grace,
In the ash, we find our place.

With every breath, we find the peace,
In silence, sweet, we find release.
Ashen serenity enfolds,
In its hush, a story told.

Night's Frigid Flame

In the dark, where shadows cling,
Fires flicker, hearts take wing.
Cold embraces warmth tonight,
In the void, we find our light.

Stars are whispers in the breeze,
Carrying tales through the trees.
Night ignites a lonely spark,
Guiding souls through endless dark.

Each flame glows, a fervent glance,
Inviting dreams to take a chance.
Frigid air, a gentle kiss,
In the cold, we find our bliss.

Dancing embers chase the chill,
Igniting passion, giving thrill.
Night's frigid flame, a mystery,
Fueling hope, setting us free.

Through the stars, the warmth expands,
Lit from within by unseen hands.
In this night, forever tame,
We embrace the frigid flame.

Warmth in the Crystal

In the heart of winter's breath,
Crystal lights begin to shine.
Each glimmer tells of hidden depth,
A warmth that's soft and divine.

Snowflakes fall like whispered dreams,
Embracing earth with tender grace.
In the silence, joy redeems,
Nature's beauty, a sweet embrace.

Hearts ignite in the twilight's glow,
Sharing secrets, hand in hand.
In the silence, love will grow,
Together, we will make our stand.

Through the night, the stars will weave,
Stories of warmth in the cold.
With each laugh, we will believe,
A joy that's timeless and bold.

When the dawn begins to rise,
Hope awakens with the light.
In the warmth beneath the skies,
Every heart takes joyful flight.

Chill of a Rogue Fire

Beneath the moon, shadows shift,
A rogue fire flickers and sings.
Whispers carried in the drift,
Chill of night with haunted flings.

Embers glow like distant stars,
Tales of ache in the dark night.
Fleeting heat hides bruised scars,
A dance of pain, a lost fight.

Winds of change, they howl and bite,
Yet hearts still flicker with dread.
A beacon in the lonely night,
Where dreams of warmth have fled.

Rogue flames flicker, tease, and play,
They hold a promise, bittersweet.
Yet in their chill, a spark will stay,
Kindling warmth in retreat.

Amidst the dark, those flames reveal,
The power of love, fierce and bright.
Through every wound, our hearts will heal,
In the chill, we find our light.

Frozen Glow of the Soul

In the stillness of the night,
Frozen echoes softly call.
A glow beneath the icy sight,
A gentle warmth, a whispered thrall.

Crystals forming on the ground,
Nature's art, a timeless score.
In their beauty, peace is found,
Reflecting light forevermore.

Hearts encased in frosted dreams,
Searching for a spark of heat.
Beneath the surface, truth redeems,
A radiant warmth, bittersweet.

Each moment holds a frozen glance,
The glow shines through the cold of night.
A dance of fate, a fleeting chance,
To embrace the warmth of light.

In this chill, our souls connect,
Bound by light, though shadows dwell.
With every heartbeat, hearts reflect,
The frozen glow within, our spell.

Spark of Icy Love

In the depths of winter's chill,
A spark ignites in frozen air.
Two hearts beat with iron will,
Defiant flames in icy glare.

Whispers dance like falling snow,
Bound by warmth in a bleak world.
As the winter winds will blow,
In our hearts, soft dreams unfurled.

Each touch ignites a tender flame,
In the cold, we find our truth.
Though the world feels stark and lame,
Our love awakens the youth.

In the silence of the night,
Frosted kisses, sweet delight.
Love as fierce as winter's bite,
Gives our souls their wings in flight.

Through the snow, our footprints blend,
A testament of two as one.
In the chill, our hearts transcend,
With a spark that can't be done.

Ember's Embrace

In the glow of twilight's flare,
Whispers dance upon the air,
Crimson flames that softly sway,
Chasing shadows far away.

Cinders floating, sparks ignite,
Dreams alight in the dark night,
Every heartbeat, warmth bestowed,
In this sanctuary, we erode.

Memories of laughter near,
Echoes of the love we share,
In the ember's soft embrace,
We find solace, find our place.

Fading light begins to fade,
Silent songs of love portrayed,
Holding close what cannot freeze,
In the fire, hearts find ease.

Hours pass, the stars awake,
Promise sealed in every wake,
Together in this sacred flame,
Two souls whisper each other's name.

Frosty Reverie

Morning breaks with icy breath,
The world adorned in winter's dress,
Glistening fields of white and blue,
A wonderland, serene and true.

Gentle flakes begin to fall,
Nature's whispers, a silent call,
Footprints trace a path so clear,
Each crystal holds a dream so dear.

Branches draped in frosty crowns,
Silent echoes of nothing sounds,
In this calm, the heart takes flight,
In chilly air, the spirit bright.

As dusk falls, a tranquil hush,
Under the stars, the world turns lush,
Each breath releases winter's song,
In frosty dreams, where hearts belong.

A moment's peace, a frozen lace,
All the worries fall from grace,
So let us dance in moon's embrace,
In this frosty reverie, find space.

Torch in a Hailstorm

Through the chaos, thunder rolls,
Tempests rage, nature consoles,
But amidst the crashing sound,
A tiny flame can still be found.

A torch that flickers, fights the chill,
In the hailstorm, it stands still,
Against the darkness, it will shine,
A beacon bright, a soul divine.

Raindrops fall like shards of sorrow,
Yet our hearts dare hope tomorrow,
For every storm that tests our might,
We gather strength, we find the light.

In the tumult, courage breeds,
Through the chaos, love still leads,
With every breath, we hold it fast,
A torch that glows, a love steadfast.

So let it rain, let tempests roar,
In the depths, we'll fight for more,
Together under skies so vast,
Our flame will shine, our bond will last.

Icy Heartbeat

In the silence of the blue,
A heartbeat drifts, so pure, so true,
Frosted air caresses skin,
Echoes where our love begins.

Shivering in the winter's hold,
Unrushed moments, tales untold,
In every breath, a story flows,
Of two hearts where the cold wind blows.

The world, a canvas stark and bright,
While we glow in warmth's delight,
In the chill, our spirits dance,
Lost together in a chance glance.

Ice and fire, a blend so rare,
Fingers entwined, a silent prayer,
In frozen veins, our pulse will race,
Together, we find our place.

Let the seasons shift and sway,
In every night, in every day,
Our icy hearts will beat as one,
In the winter light, where love begun.

Fire Within the Ice

Frozen surface, secrets lie,
Whispers echo, cold winds sigh.
A flame that flickers, soft yet bright,
Heart ablaze in wintry night.

Beneath the chill, a warmth concealed,
In frozen hearts, love is revealed.
A dance of sparks, the ice will bend,
A tale of hope, where sparks descend.

Snowflakes fall on crimson hue,
Embers glow with a vibrant view.
In this realm of frost and fire,
Yearning souls ignite desire.

With each breath, the tension grows,
In icy grasp, passion flows.
Hearts entwined in frigid clutches,
Through the cold, their spirit touches.

In shadows cast by pale moonlight,
The warmth of fire ignites their plight.
Together they weather the frigid storm,
In frozen dreams, they find their form.

Cerulean Heat

Beneath the skies of azure blue,
Where sunbeams dance and shadows strew.
The world ignites, a vibrant flare,
Heatwaves shimmer, summer's dare.

Waves crash down on golden sand,
Touch of warmth, a lover's hand.
Blue horizons stretch beyond sight,
Inviting hearts to burn so bright.

On cerulean nights, desires bloom,
In fragrant gardens, lovers loom.
The air is thick with passion's sigh,
Underneath the vast starlit sky.

Cascading laughter fills the air,
In this heated realm, none compare.
Drawing closer, souls entwined,
In cerulean dreams, love defined.

The sun dips low, painting the scene,
With hues of red, and vibrant green.
In twilight's breath, heartbeats race,
In every glance, the spark of grace.

Embers Beneath the Snow

Silent whispers in the night,
Frozen world, cloaked in white.
Yet below, a warmth resides,
Where hidden embers softly bide.

Snowflakes blanket stories old,
In crispy silence, tales unfold.
A flicker here, a spark in sight,
Eyes alight with hidden plight.

Frosty breath and winter's chill,
Yet in the heart, a burning thrill.
With every flake that falls so slow,
A promise blooms, the fire's glow.

Together in this snowy scene,
Two souls merge, a bond serene.
Underneath the frost and frost,
Their whispered hopes, they cannot cost.

As winter wanes, and spring draws near,
The embers rise, no place for fear.
Through frozen nights, a love will grow,
Transforming snow to vibrant glow.

Shivering Heatwave

In the midst of summer's blaze,
Heatwaves dance in swelter's haze.
A paradox of warmth and chill,
Where hearts race fast but souls stand still.

Air electric, charged with glee,
Shivering dreams start to flee.
The sun above, a fierce delight,
But shadows linger, stealing light.

Ocean breezes whisper low,
In sweltering heat, passions grow.
Fingers brush in sultry tease,
In this spell, they find their ease.

Through the gloom, sparks start to fly,
With every glance, the truth draws nigh.
Hot and cold, a thrilling race,
Caught in love's sweet, dizzying chase.

A shiver runs down warm skin's path,
In the heart, both fire and wrath.
Together they steer through heat's embrace,
In this wild dance, they find their place.